Health
and
Healing

Lilian B. Yeomans, M.D.

GOSPEL PUBLISHING HOUSE
Springfield, Missouri
02-0732

Contents

HEALTH AND HEALING
(Formerly published as *The Royal Road to Health-Ville*)
Copyright 1938, 1966
Revised Edition Published 1973
by the
Gospel Publishing House
Springfield, Missouri 65802
Printed in the United States of America
5th Printing 1992
ISBN 0-88243-732-1

1

The Human Body

Not long ago I was staying with a friend who is a fine cook. She would go into her kitchen and after a very short time come out with a beautiful fluffy cake, a chiffon pie, or a pan of lovely rolls. I followed her into the kitchen one day to find out how she did it, and what do you suppose I saw? Beautiful appliances, all white enamel and glittering chromium. They were puzzles to me. I would not have known what to do with them or how to take care of them. But the riddle was solved when I found that with each appliance the maker had provided a book of instructions that had to be carefully studied and faithfully followed if you were to have rolls light as feathers and pies and cakes that made people's mouths water just to look at them. The books with the appliances told what they were made to do, and warned the owner against misusing them. Also they gave the names and addresses of the makers so that they could be sent for to make repairs or put in new parts when needed.

3

You have of your very own a machine so wonderful that the most costly ones made by men are just tinsel toys from the dime store in comparison with it. That machine is your body. Man-made machines may look all right at a distance, but when you get close to them you always find flaws and defects. But this machine I am telling you about now is more beautiful the nearer you get to it, and if you magnify it four or five hundred times it is found to be made of rich tissues arranged in lovely patterns. The tissues in their turn are made of tiny cells of different shapes (some are star-shaped) all of them beautiful. The cells are different because they have different tasks to perform, and they all work together for the good of the whole. For in this machine, the most wonderful of God's works in the material universe, His law is, "No schism in the body" (1 Corinthians 12:25).

Your body was made expressly for you by God Himself. It was not turned out with thousands of others like buttons from a factory. God tells us that all our members were written in His book "when as yet there was none of them" (Psalm 139:14, 16). The wisest men confess that they never expect to be able to find out all the secrets of this wonderful living machine. (As you use it don't forget that it is a love gift from God. Say to yourself, "God thought of me and loved me, so I am here.") Over this machine, worth more than all the millions in the world, God has given you control.

NOTE: You will notice that I give chapter and verse for everything I tell you. I hope you will look up these references in your Bible. Then this little book will be a great blessing to you for it will teach you how to use the Bible when you need to be healed, or when you have to pray for sick people. The only medicine God gives us is His Word. He says, "He sent His Word, and healed them" (Psalm 107:20).

Count some of the treasures you own and see how rich you are. There is the most marvelous engine pump ever known — the heart. It never goes on strike but forces pure blood through pipes to every cell in the body, feeding muscles, bones, and nerves; working day and night, even when you are fast asleep, as long as you live. The blood gathers up worn out matter as it goes, and takes it to the right side of the heart from which it is pumped into the lungs to be made pure again by the air we breathe. Then it is sent back to the left side of the heart from which it is pumped again to the millions of cells that are always waiting for the dinner bell to ring.

I wonder if you know that you have a pair of self-adjusting telescopes in your body. Some of the telescopes men make have to be moved and changed by heavy machinery to focus on objects at different distances, but you can look up from darning socks to watch a silver cloud sailing across the blue sky with *your* telescopes. Even a child can do this. Your wonderful telescopes adjust themselves!

We live in an age when it seems everybody has a camera. Some camera enthusiasts have extensive outfits that amaze most of us. They have close-up lens, telephoto lens, all types of light filters, films for different situations, light meters, and many other accessories, all designed to improve the quality of pictures. But God has placed in your body the smallest cameras in the world, your two eyes. Did you know they are taking pictures all the time? The images these cameras make on the rear wall of your eyes are carried to your brain and you *see*. Only God, who made you, knows exactly how this is done. But wonders do not stop there. You have in your brain an art gallery called memory in which some of these pictures are hung, never to be removed while you live. You will agree with me that all the wealth in the world would not buy some of them; for instance, your mother's tender face and the baby sweetness of your children. With them you are rich.

In order to make no mistakes about the use to which you should put your wonderful body, you must study your book of instructions, the Bible, every day.

As I said, God has placed your body under your control. But He has taught you very plainly what He made it for, and that is His own glory.

He tells us that the things we cannot see are shown to us by the things we *can* see (Romans 1: 19, 20). We cannot see God, yet as we look at the mountains, oceans, stars, and flowers, as well as many other things God made, His strength, power, majesty, and beauty are seen in them. But when it comes to man, God can unveil Himself much more fully than through rocks, stars, oceans, and flowers. Man is made in God's image and so formed that God can dwell in his body and shine His glory through it. He can speak with man's tongue, think through his mind and love in his heart. In that way we can glorify God with our "bodies which are His" (1 Corinthians 6:20).

To glorify means to make glorious. We cannot add to God's glory, but we can let those who look at us see it shining through our bodies. Doesn't it make you glad that you have a body that can be used to make men see the glory of God?

Let me tell you some things you will find in the Bible about man's body (1 Corinthians 6:13-20).

1. It is the Lord's. He claims it for Himself.

2. He loves it so much that He is going to raise it from the dead.

3. It is a member of Christ.

4. It is the temple of the Holy Spirit.

5. It was bought with a price.

6. When the Lord Jesus Christ comes to take those who are in Jesus to be forever with Him, their bodies are to be changed and made like unto His glorious body (1 John 3:2).

I have always admired the beautiful body God made for man. Perhaps because when I was still very young I studied it so closely. Preparing to be a doctor, I had to know every bone, muscle, nerve, and blood vessel. The more I studied it, the more wonderful it seemed. I was not saved then and the first time I saw a human brain it made God so real to me that I was afraid. When I thought of what the brain of man had done, I could not help thinking how mighty the One who made it must be. And I was afraid! But when I came to Jesus I learned to love Him so that I was no longer afraid, for I knew my sins were washed away in the precious Blood that He shed for me on Calvary. Have you that knowledge? If not repent and believe the gospel (John 3:16), for only in the strength that God supplies through His eternal Son can you glorify God in your body and your Spirit which are His.

My friend, the good cook I told you about, is able to do such good work because she knows how to use her appliances as the makers intended them to be used. She carefully studies the books of instruction to find out what to do and what not to do and obeys every rule. That is why she can feed her friends such good things. If we will do that with our book of instructions, the Bible, the Word of God, we shall be able to use our bodies to glorify God and help every one with whom we come in contact. We shall feed the hungry with the living Bread that came down from heaven so that they will hunger no more.

In the first book in the Bible, Genesis, we are told how God made our bodies (Genesis 1:26). He who is three in one, Father, Son, and Holy Spirit, made us in His own image and likeness. Likewise, man is in three parts, spirit, soul, and body (1 Thessalonians 5:23).

Before this, God had created many wonderful and beautiful things, trees, plants, flowers, great whales, fish, animals, and birds. The air was filled with the scent of blossoms, the whir of swift wings, and the music of bird songs.

But when He made man He did not form him like any of these. He made him like Himself, God-like, *like God*. And God gave man dominion over His works. He was the ruler of them all. After all was done God looked at His work and said it was "very good" (Genesis 1:31).

How fine the body of the first man was! God called it "very good." That means every part of it was perfect. No trace of sickness or weakness. Not the slightest blemish upon it. Our first father, Adam, walked this earth in a body fit for the king that he was. God gave him work to do that no man living today could do. He was told to name all the animals, and as they passed meekly before him he gave to each bird and beast the right name (Genesis 2:19,

20.) What a brain he had to be able to do that! How strong he was to stand such a strain on mind and body!

Now I know the question that you want to ask. It is, "Why are we not like that today? Almost everybody I know has something wrong with them. It is nothing but sickness, sickness everywhere. Can you explain it?"

Yes. The book of instructions, the Bible, tells us all about it. Sickness came because the first man failed to obey the rules God had given him about his body, the wonderful living machine.

In the garden in which God placed Adam (the most beautiful garden that ever was, because the Lord planted it), there were all sorts of trees bearing luscious fruits. Man could enjoy the most delicious meals, for God told him that there was no limit. Of every tree, excepting one, he might freely eat. But if he dared to disobey and eat of the fruit of the forbidden tree, God told him he would surely die (Genesis 2:16, 17).

Man disobeyed and dared to take into the wonderful living machine what God had forbidden him to eat; and through his sin, disease and death came to him and all of his children down to this day. That is the cause of every case of sickness you see. There was no disease till man sinned. It was not known on earth till then.

From that sad day tiny babies come into the world with bodies that are apt to get sick. Sometimes they are even born with some awful disease in their blood.

People sometimes bring sickness upon themselves by their own sins; for, as with Adam, sin and sickness go together. There were two men who were called Mr. Chang and Mr. Eng. If you asked one to dinner the other came whether you wanted him or not. They were the famous Siamese Twins who were joined by a band of flesh that could not be cut without killing them. Sin and sickness are like that. If you invite sin, sickness comes along.

2

A Promise and a Covering

If Satan, who tempted Eve to eat the forbidden fruit and share it with Adam, tempts you to do wrong, you need not yield. We are warned that he goes about like a roaring lion seeking whom he may devour. One way he devours those who yield to him is by eating up their flesh with terrible sicknesses so that they are just skin and bone. The Bible tells us to "resist" him and he will flee from us (James 4:7).

Obey your book of instructions and you will be kept, body, soul, and spirit by the power of God.

A little old hymn — I wonder if you ever sang it when you were a tiny tot in Sunday school — tells how this may be done.

> Yield not to temptation
>   For yielding is sin,
> Each victory will help you
>   Some other to win.
> Fight manfully onward,
>   Dark passions subdue,
> Look ever to Jesus,
>   He will carry you through.

Now we find God in the cool of the day going to the beautiful garden He had made for man's first home to visit Adam and Eve. But alas they were nowhere to be found. Instead of running to the One who had so loved them and given them such precious things, they ran away from Him and hid among the trees of the garden. As He called Adam by name, they came trembling and afraid; for they had sinned and told the saddest story earth has ever heard – the story of the Fall. They stood ashamed and helpless before God. They had listened to Satan and disobeyed their Maker.

The awful sentence was pronounced, the death sentence. "The soul that sinneth it shall die" (Ezekiel 18:4). God always keeps His Word and He had warned them that if they ate of the forbidden fruit they would surely die (Romans 6:23). So He said to them "Unto dust shalt thou return" (Genesis 3:19).

Right then and there death began to work in those wonderful living machines, their bodies. From that time sickness, which is just slow dying, began to be seen and felt by the children of men.

But even then God did not forsake them. He gave them two wonderful things, a promise, and a covering.

The promise was that there was to come one glad day a virgin-born Son, the "seed of the woman," who was to destroy the old serpent who had deceived Eve, by bruising his head (Genesis 3:15; 3:21). When a serpent's head is mashed, that is the end of the serpent.

This was partly fulfilled when the Lord Jesus Christ was born in Bethlehem of Judaea of the Virgin Mary. Then when the Lord Jesus was crucified on

Calvary, Satan was brought to naught and his power over all who trust in the precious blood of Jesus, was broken (Hebrews 2:14).

The second precious gift was a covering (coats) which God Himself made and put on them because without them they could never dwell in His presence. What were these coats made of?

For the first time, suffering and death entered that beautiful Garden of Eden. Innocent animals cried in anguish as their lives were sacrificed and their blood shed. Of their beautiful skins God fashioned coats for Adam and Eve. Those coats covered them, spirit, soul, and body. They are a picture of Christ made unto us righteousness (rightness) when He died on the cross to redeem us (1 Corinthians 1:30). He made us right in spirit, soul, and body. And a right body is a healthy body.

When disease began to show itself in the bodies of men (because the Fall had made them apt to get sick), God told them to pray to Him in faith in the Christ who was to come and die for them, and He would heal them.

In the Book of Beginnings, Genesis, we have the story of a king, Abimelech by name, who was stricken with a sore sickness in his own body, as well as among the members of his family, because he had taken another man's wife, intending to make her his wife (Genesis 20:7, 17). He did not know that she was Abraham's wife or he would not have done it; but he had done wrong to take her, and God told him that if he did not make the wrong right he would surely die and all his family with him. God promised him healing if he obeyed and told him exactly how to obtain it.

(You will remember that I told you that this book of instructions tells us how to have the wonderful living machines repaired by their Maker; so listen carefully for God says, "I am the Lord, I change not") (Malachi 3:6).

God told Abimelech that he must first make restitution by taking Sarah back to her own husband and then have her husband, Abraham, pray for him that he might be healed.

Abraham trusted in the Lord Jesus Christ. He spoke of Him as the Lamb of God and saw Him *by faith* though He had not come yet. The Lord Jesus said Himself, "Abraham rejoiced to see my day; and he saw it and was glad" (John 8:56).

So it was by faith in the Name of the Lord Jesus Christ that Abimelech was healed all those thousands of years ago, and it is by faith in that same Name that the sick are made well today. We who believe are told to lay our hands on sick people in the Name of the Lord Jesus and they will recover (Mark 16:15-18; James 5:14-16). Just after the Lord Jesus gave this command in Mark He was caught up into heaven and sat on the right hand of God.

God never changes and never will change. We are just as sure of healing as Abimelech was if we go about it as he did, according to our book of instructions, the Bible.

I was on the platform of a church where I had been asked to pray for the sick and, as I was talking to them and telling them from the Bible that God would heal them if they came His way, I happened to look at the ministers on the platform with me. There were three besides myself, one woman and two men. I had known all of them for many years and positively

knew that all four of us would have been under the
ground for many years if God didn't heal just the
same as He did thousands of years ago.

One of them had diabetes mellitus. Doctors had
pronounced the death sentence. He was told that he
could pass into a stupor and die any moment and
must never be left alone. He became blind from the
disease. He was prayed for just as Abimelech was,
not by Abraham but by a daughter of Abraham who
by faith saw the Lamb of God dying for our sins and
sicknesses. He was made well and has been working
for the Lord ever since — about six years.

The other brother had stone in the kidney. He
suffered absolute agony and his friends sent an ambulance and surgeons who said he must be removed
to the hospital at once. He said he could and would
trust God. His wife stood with him in faith and believers were sent for to pray for his healing. That was
about four years ago and he has been perfectly well
and active for his Master ever since.

The sister who was with us had had seven serious
operations by some of the greatest surgeons in the
United States. At last she heard of Jesus of Nazareth
and was prayed for and healed, though the doctors
(on whom a small fortune had been spent) said
there was no hope.

I was dying the morphine death 40 years ago, and
had nothing to look forward to but a funeral, and
not much of one at that. No one could help me but
God, and at last I found the way to Him. It was just
the same old path that Abimelech trod, repentance
and faith in the Lamb of God; and it brought the
same results. *It never fails.*

3

Healing Pictures in the Bible

Books of instructions sent with machines are well illustrated. People, especially children, learn more easily from pictures than in any other way. They will turn over the leaves of a picture book for hours, and teachers find that the time is well spent if the book is a good one.

God has placed many beautiful pictures in the Bible, our book of instructions. From some of these we learn how to be free from sickness. Let us look at the picture of the Passover Lamb in Exodus 12.

The great-grandchildren of Abraham came down to Egypt to live because there was no food in Canaan. They had a very hard time there for the Egyptians were cruel to them. Worse still, they failed to do some things the God of their fathers had told them to do. But when they cried to God, He was merciful and took them out of Egypt to lead them to a new home. When the king of Egypt, who was very strong with his army and war chariots, would not let them go (though God told him to), God warned him that He would send an awful plague that would leave one dead in every house.

But before God did this he told Moses, His servant, to tell the children of Israel (as they were called) what to do to keep the plague away ·from their homes.

The father of each house was told to take a pure, spotless lamb without any flaw in it for himself and his children. I can see the picture; can't you? The little ones gather round as the father brings in the lovely little creature, and cry, "Oh, isn't it snow white! May I have it, Father? Its coat is as soft as down. I want it for a pet."

But the father shakes his head sadly, "No, my child, you may not have the little lamb."

"What are you going to do with it, Father?"

"I am going to kill it and put its blood on the door so that when the death angel comes to our house he will pass over it. This night he is bringing death to every home on which there is no blood."

"O Father, must the lamb die?"

"Yes, it must die that you may live."

And that night there was a great cry in all the land of Egypt, for there was not a house where there was not one dead. But in the blood-marked homes of the children of Israel, all was well. Not so much as one tiny child sick. And Paul the apostle tells us that in this scene we have a picture of what the Lamb of God does for those who trust Him, for he says, "Christ our passover is sacrificed for us" (1 Corinthians 5:7).

> Beneath the blood-stained lintel
> I, and my children, stand.

A messenger of evil is flying through the land.
   There is no other refuge from the destroyer's
      face.
Beneath the blood-stained lintel
   Shall be our hiding place.

I knew a lady who had a very large and very sickly family. People used to joke because there seemed to be almost always a placard on the house with measles or scarlet fever or chicken pox (once it was small pox). But it was no joke to the lady, for she had so many children that it took a great deal of her time to nurse them through these awful sicknesses; and besides, she loved her boys and girls and feared she might lose them.

About that time God was pouring out His Holy Spirit on us in that town and some of us were praying and reading our Bibles day and night. This poor mother heard of our meetings and crept in one day. She told us her troubles and we talked to her about the Lamb of God who bore all our sins and sickness. We said, "Put the Blood on the door and it will keep these plagues away. But you and the children must feed on the Lord Jesus in the Word, as the children of Israel ate the flesh of the Passover Lamb." She did what we said.

I knew her for years after that and she never had another health department card on her house. She read and read the book of instructions and taught it to others so that sick people used to go to her house (the blood of the Lamb of God was on the door) to be made well through prayer, just as Abimelech went to Abraham. And many of them were healed.

When the awful influenza plague was killing its millions and almost every house bore a placard, my sister, Amy Yeomans, said to everybody she could reach, "There will never be a placard on our home. Not because we are any better than anyone else, but because the Blood is on the door and the destroying angel must pass over. God said so." She made her boast *in the Lord* and God honored His own Word. I visited some stricken ones that sent for me, but it never entered our home.

After the Passover, Pharaoh was in a hurry to get the children of Israel away. The Egyptians were so frightened at what had happened in their homes that they gave them silver and gold, as well as clothing to help them on their journey. They took food, but Moses, who was a doctor (Acts 7:22), did not take any drugs but trusted God to keep them from disease as He did during the terrible plague that killed the Egyptians. And the Bible says that there was not one feeble one among them (Psalm 105:37). All were ready for the day's march and set out with shining faces and shoulders squared.

When they came to the Red Sea, God rolled it away; and they walked over on dry land and sang a hymn of praise to God on the other side. When Pharaoh tried to follow them to take them back to Egypt (he was sorry he had let them get away), he and all his host and chariots were buried in the Red Sea which came rolling back when God's people were safely over.

Now we shall look at another picture. Let us call it "The Wonderful Tree."

When the Israelites had gone some distance they met a great trial. The water was so bitter that though they were thirsty, they could not drink it (Exodus 15:

23, 24). Sometimes very bitter water makes you sick at the stomach.

I am sorry to say that they did a very wrong thing. They complained against Moses who had been sent by God to deliver them from the iron furnace of Egypt. Over and over again in the book of instructions we are warned that if we misuse our tongues, which God gave us to glorify Him, we shall be sick (Proverbs 13:3).

But if they did the wrong thing, Moses did the right thing, for he cried to God. And God did the most wonderful thing for them. He showed Moses a tree! It was a wonderful tree, and it was there all the time; but even Moses did not see just how wonderful it was till God showed it to him. He told him to throw this tree into the waters and they would become sweet. And sure enough, when the poor people with their tongues cleaving to the roofs of their mouths for dryness dared to take a drink, it was sweet to their taste. Oh, how they drank and drank of the sparkling water! And right there God gave them a promise which still stands and will stand forever, for God does not change. We call it the "Covenant of Healing." As you know, a covenant is a solemn pact or bargain.

It says, "If thou wilt diligently hearken to the voice of the Lord thy God, and wilt do that which is right in his sight, and wilt give ear to his commandments, and keep all his statutes, I will put none of these diseases upon thee, which I have brought upon the Egyptians: for I am the Lord that healeth thee" (Exodus 15:26).

Water is a type of life. Our bodies are largely made up of it. But the water of human life is bitter at its very source because of sin. Even a new born baby may get sick and die. It may be born sickly. There is only one thing that can make life's water pure and sweet, free from sin, sickness, and other defilement; and that is the Tree. Do you ask, "Oh, tell me where it grows! I want to find it and cast it into my life for the bitterness of sin and sickness is more than I can bear. What shall I do?" Exactly what Moses did. Cry unto the Lord and He will show you the cross on Calvary's hill with One hanging on it, dying under the double burden of your sins and sickness (John 1:29). A great prophet saw it seven hundred years before Jesus Christ was born in Bethlehem and cried, "Surely He hath borne our diseases and carried our pains" (Isaiah 53:4, literal translation).

When the Lord Jesus Christ came and lived on earth seven hundred years after this was written about Him, the evangelist Matthew tells us that when they brought sick people to Him, He healed them *all*, that this word of the prophet might be fulfilled (Matthew 8:17). It had to be fulfilled because it was the word God put into his mouth. It has to be fulfilled today, for God cannot lie.

Remember, you must cast the Tree into the water of your life by looking at the cross of Calvary and believing God who says, "I am the Lord that healeth thee."

4

Songs of Inspiration

I want to turn to the wonderful lessons about our bodies which we learn from *songs* in the Bible. Yes, the most wonderful songs that have ever been sung are in our book of instructions. That may well be, for they are not of earth but of heaven. The Holy Spirit sang them through men's lips.

Does it seem strange to teach from songs? It is really a very old way of teaching and has never gone altogether out of fashion. Moses taught the children of Israel a song which he commanded them to teach to their children for all time. They were to have it in their mouths and never to forget it. It tells of the faithfulness of God to His people and their unfaithfulness to Him.

But the "Sweet Singer of Israel" was David, who was also a prophet and king. He had some very hard attacks of sickness and learned how to pray and sing himself well again. Some of the songs he sang have been the means of making many other sick people well. That is because they are God's words, and He says, "He sent his word, and healed them" (Psalm 107:20).

One lesson that David teaches us from his own experience is very important, and that is that we must humble ourselves and confess our sins when seeking to be made well. He says in one psalm that when he kept silence about his sins, "his bones rotted away," and he was "roaring all the day" (Psalm 32:3). How he must have suffered! There is an old proverb which says, "He who will not speak his sin to God has to groan." Another says, "A dumb conscience makes a loud voiced pain." But when he said "I will confess . . . to Jehovah," we find him "compassed about with songs of deliverance." No more rotten bones and roaring, but glad praises to God for healing. Fully recovered from his awful disease he turns round and calls upon us all to "be glad in the Lord and rejoice . . . and shout for joy, all ye that are righteous in heart" (Psalm 32:11).

When I was a child I was afraid to have my Mother line me up before the doctor for he always said, "Put out your tongue." And when I put it out it seemed to tell him all the naughty things I had done. For he would say, "This child has been eating trash," though I had not told him one thing about the candy I had had and the extra piece of pie I had begged from the old cook. But he knew the signs of a healthy tongue, and when mine wasn't healthy he would make me go to bed early and worst of all, take a dose of castor oil before I went.

David gives us the signs of a healthy tongue for the Christian; and they are, first, confession of wrong-doing when our consciences tell us that we have sinned. Second, a testimony to Christ, and third, praise and more praise. Why he calls his tongue "glory"! (Psalm 30:12). If the name of yours is "grouch" you had better have it changed to "glory."

One of the songs he sang is "The Lord Is My Shepherd." It is a portrait of Jesus Christ, the Good Shepherd, who laid down His life for the sheep that they might have life and have it more abundantly. Those who have abundant life, great vitality, are well because the healthy body fights off disease.

This song of the Good Shepherd has been sung in more places by more different kinds of people, than any other song. When we read or sing it or listen to it being sung, we should remember that the health of the sheep is the Shepherd's care. He does not trust the sheep and lambs to keep themselves well, but at their cry is always ready to heal them. The Good Shepherd is not only ready but able also to make you perfectly well if you will call on Him. David says, "O Lord my God, I cried unto thee and thou hast healed me" (Psalm 30:2).

God is the only One who can heal every disease. The greatest doctors will tell you that there are cases of sickness for which they can do nothing. Sometimes people who are not very well off think if they had plenty of money they could get cured. But this is not always so. I have known those who spent fortunes trying to find health. Some of them went to the finest surgeons who told them that there was no hope. Others tried climates, took all kinds of cures, dieted till they were nearly starved, with no results.

But God says that He heals *all* our diseases just as He forgives all our sins. You will find this in one of the psalms of David, "Who forgiveth all thine iniquities, who healeth all thy diseases" (Psalm 103:3).

Some who have tried everything else in vain have called upon Him and proved that He says what He means and does what He says.

In some Psalms David teaches us of the tender watch care of God over His own. Psalm 121 has been called by some who have proved its truth "The Sleepless Sentry." It says that the Lord "who neither slumbers nor sleeps" shall preserve us from all evil. That means sickness, as well as other things, for sickness is part of the curse upon those who break God's law (Deuteronomy 28:58-61).

There is a beautiful Psalm which God's people dearly love. I have heard a congregation of those who had been healed by faith in the Lord Jesus Christ or who were seeking divine healing repeating it together. Every one of them knew it by heart. (It is a very good thing to commit verses about the Lord's healing to memory.) God tells us that if we attend to His words, listen to them, keep them before our eyes, and hide them in the midst of our hearts, they are "health to all our flesh" (Proverbs 4:20-22).

The Psalm the whole congregation was saying from memory is called by some, "The Hiding Place," because it tells of a place where we may hide so that no sickness can find us, not even the most contagious pestilence (Psalm 91:10). Do you long to know where that safe shelter is? I can tell you, for God gives it in the book of instructions. You will find it in Psalm 31:20: "Thou shalt hide them in the secret of thy presence." That is what our Lord Jesus Christ meant when He said "Abide in me" (John 15:4). The great apostle Paul could say, "For me to live is Christ" (Philippians 1:21). He tells us to follow his example so this was not for apostles only (Philippians 3:17).

If you lived in a poor little house in a dangerous place where evil persons might break in any moment to do you and your loved ones grievous harm, and were invited into the finest palace on earth where you and yours would be safely guarded night and day, wouldn't you move at once?

Of course you would. That is exactly what God offers you and yours, for this wonderful salvation, which includes the body, is for your "house," meaning your family as well as yourself personally.

The 91st Psalm says of those who live in the Hiding Place, which is Jesus Christ, "There shall no evil befall thee, neither shall any plague come nigh thy dwelling" (Psalm 91:10).

Let me tell you right here about how God made this word good to one who trusted Him to do so. A Christian business man, who trusted God for his family as well as for himself, was away on a trip of inspection for his company. During his absence which lasted some time, one of his children, a daughter who is now an ordained minister, was taken ill. In his absence a very fine physician was called who at once pronounced the case as diphtheria and ordered all the usual precautions, including a rigid quarantine.

Just as this was about to be carried out, the father returned. As soon as he heard the sad news he took to prayer. (I did not see him do it, but am as certain as if I had for he *always prayed over everything.*) After prayer he rose from his knees filled with courage and faith. Going straight to the doctor he said, "Doctor I learn that you have ordered my house into quarantine for diphtheria." The doctor said, "I am sorry to say that is the case. Little Ruth has the disease." "I beg your pardon, Doctor, but I have to tell you that there is no diphtheria in my house. It is impossible for it to be there." The Doctor gazed at him as though he thought he had gone mad.

"I have a question to ask you, Doctor. Was a swab taken from the child's throat and sent to the Provincial Laboratory?"

"No. It was unnecessary. The case is a clear one of diphtheria."

The Bible says that if we constantly think about God's word we have more understanding than our teachers, and so it proved with my friend for he asked, "As the child's father, have I not a legal right to insist upon the laboratory test before my house is quarantined?"

The doctor had to yield to this, and after carefully swabbing the throat, sent the specimen to the laboratory. The report came back "negative," and there was no serious illness. In answer to prayer the child was running round as well as ever in a day or two; and needless to say, there was no quarantine.

I am thinking as I remember this case of a beautiful psalm which shows us God's thought for the family. If you note it carefully you will see that it includes health for every one in the home.

I love to call it the "Home Sweet Home Psalm" — number 128. Read it with me and first of all see that it is for "*everyone* that feareth the Lord" (verse 1). That means to fear Him as you feared your father, if you had a good one, too much to willingly disobey him. You feared him because you knew he was so good that he would have to punish you if you did wrong. But you loved him for that very goodness which made him so careful to train you in the right way.

Verse 2 promises the father health and strength to earn a living for himself and family and a good appetite to enjoy what he had earned.

Verse 3 tells of a healthy mother and "children like olive plants" round the table.

Verse 6 promises this man long life and "children's children" playing round his feet.

If we only had more homes like that, how much better it would be for everybody!

There is a very joyful psalm that people who have been healed by faith in the Lord Jesus Christ love to use in praising God. It is Psalm 30. David has been very sick; has gone down to the grave; but God has in mercy brought him up in answer to his prayer. "O Lord my God, I cried unto thee, and thou hast healed me" (Psalm 30:2).

He is so happy about it that he asks all God's people to help him praise (verse 4). In the 11th verse he says that the Lord has girded him with gladness and turned his mourning into dancing.

Some people think it is very wrong to dance in worshiping God, but David got so full of glory sometimes that he had to praise God with every muscle in his body. Do you remember how he danced before the Lord "with all his might," when he brought up the Ark of God to the city of David? (2 Samuel 6: 14).

5

Will the Lord Heal Me?

In the last book of the Old Testament written by the prophet Malachi (his name means the messenger of Jehovah), we read of a glorious sunrise of which God gave him a vision. It was a very dark age, and perhaps the messenger was almost ready to give up hope. But God knew how to cheer his heart and the hearts of others who were longing for the coming of the Christ. He said, "Unto you that fear my name shall the Sun of righteousness arise with healing in His wings; and ye shall go forth, and grow up as calves of the stall" (Malachi 4:2).

It was four long dark centuries before this Word came true in the coming of the Lord Jesus Christ, the Light of the world, who cried to men, "He that followeth me shall not walk in darkness but shall have the light of life" (John 8:12).

"That was the true light, which lighteth every man that cometh into the world." All we have to do is to get close enough to Him and we shall find healing in His wings.

To get the light and warmth of the sun you have to turn toward it like the sunflower, which always looks sunward. So we must look to the Lamb of God for healing. Let the blessed rays of divine light and life play all through your whole being.

One of the most wonderful healings I ever saw was given through this "Sunrise" Scripture — Malachi 4:2. A Baptist minister, whose wife was a beloved sister in Christ, was very sick. He had a deep seated abscess — or pocket full of pus — under his tongue. His throat, tongue, and all the parts near by were swollen to many times their normal size. His tongue was so large that it would not stay in his mouth but hung out, a large purple mass. He could not swallow, or say one word. He was in awful pain. They had a very good surgeon, but he would not operate because he said it was too dangerous. He said he would watch the case for a while but could not promise that the man would live. The minister and his wife had been believers in divine healing; and when they saw that all human hope was gone, they made up their minds to cast themselves on the Great Physician. So the wife asked the doctor for his bill. He said, "I do not want to give you a bill, I have done nothing for you. I would rather wait and see if I can operate." The minister's wife said, "But Doctor, we are sure you have done your best and we want to pay you. You would be willing to say that everything had been done that could be done, would you not?" "Yes," said the doctor, "but I would rather not take any money." The wife insisted and said, "We are going to have another doctor." "Well let me call him in consultation." "This doctor does not consult with other doctors." "He has to," said the doctor, "the law demands it." And then the wife said, "Our new doctor is the Lord Jesus."

So that night some believers were sent for to pray for the man. After prayer I begged the sister to go to bed because she had not had any sleep for many nights. I told her to believe God for a real healing. Just then the Lord flashed this verse (Malachi 4:2) into my mind and said, "Give it to her and tell her to believe it." It seemed almost heartless to talk about "gambolling like a calf" when her husband was so far gone, but that was the reading in the margin of my Bible and I gave it to her. She pillowed her head on this Word of God and went to sleep.

A brother took care of the groaning sick man. After a while the Lord said to the brother who was acting as nurse, "Sit on his bed and make him rest his head on your breast. I will give him sleep."

This was done and the brother dimmed the light. In a few moments the sick man was fast asleep. He had not slept for many nights. As the brother supported the sick man's head, he rested his own head on God's Word. In twenty minutes he smelled the most awful odor he had ever smelled. Turning up the light he found the whole bed, and all their clothing, simply soaked in vile smelling, poisonous pus. God had operated and removed the poison. The sick man wakened perfectly well and together they had a bonfire and burned up everything, even the mattress. Then they scrubbed the place, and when the little wife wakened she had a well husband who was hungry for breakfast. A year or so afterwards when they had moved out of town, the minister made a great big sled on which he used to draw his wife to church. It was a bright winter's day and he played that he was a skittish colt and kicked up his heels. Then the Lord said to the wife, "What is that?" And she remembered the Word of God which promised that he should go forth and gambol, or play, like a calf.

That Word has never lost its power, as the Baptist minister proved for himself. But we have to be very careful when we are trusting God's Word to make sure that we are in the place where we can claim it for our own.

This promise is addressed to those who "fear my name," God's name, and that means that we ask in submission to His will. Indeed it is because we see in the Book of instructions that it is His will that our bodies should be strong and healthy, that we feel it to be our duty to ask Him to heal us.

Then this promise is for those who have childlike confidence, like the apostle John who lay on Jesus' breast. To receive the healing we must draw near to His heart of love, get under His very wings.

The Lord Jesus said in His sad farewell to Jerusalem, "How often would I have gathered thy children together, even as a hen gathereth her chickens under her wings, and ye would not" (Matthew 23: 37). Let us be as simple as little chickens and nestle under His great strong wings. No disease can enter there.

It is so much easier for us than it was for those in Malachi's time, for his vision has come to pass. The Lord Jesus Christ was made man and dwelt among us. We have beheld His glory. He was crucified for us and buried, but death could not hold Him, and He rose from the dead and ascended to the right hand of God where He is exalted, and He hath shed forth the Holy Spirit upon those who believe.

Through men like Matthew, Mark, Luke, John, Paul, and others, the Holy Spirit has given us the wondrous story of the life of the Lord Jesus Christ. We find Him going about "healing all that were oppressed of the devil" (Acts 10:38).

One time He came into a synagogue on the sabbath to teach and saw there a poor woman who was bent double and could not lift herself up.

And He called her to Him. That is the first step, get near to Him. It was very hard for her to come, deformed as she was and unable to lift up her head. It was very humiliating too, and to make it harder for her, the ruler of the synagogue was angry and did not want her healed on the sabbath day. But she came to Jesus. Don't let anything keep you from coming to Him.

And the Lord Jesus said, "Woman, thou art loosed from thine infirmity," and He laid His hands upon her and immediately she was made straight and glorified God (Luke 13:10-17).

When the ruler of the synagogue spoke angrily because the Lord Jesus Christ had made this woman well on the sabbath day, the Lord said, "Doth not each one of you on the sabbath loose his ox or his ass from the stall and lead him away to watering? Ought not this woman, being a daughter of Abraham, whom Satan hath bound, lo, these eighteen years, be loosed from this bond on the sabbath day?" So Jesus said she ought to be healed, and He loves you just as much as He loved her and died to take your sins and sicknesses away just as much as hers. If you "ought to be healed," whose fault is it if you stay sick? Not the fault of the Lord Jesus. He bore your sickness and sin on the Cross and all you have to do is to take pardon and healing. I was called to pray for a neighbor lady who was suffering a great deal. She is saved and has the Baptism in the Holy Spirit, as in Acts 2: 4, but she was in such pain and felt so weary of suffering that she hardly seemed to want to get well. But I told her this great truth from the lips of the Lord Himself that she *ought* to get well. It was her duty, I told her. And she saw that she owed it to her Lord to be well and go about her Father's business. So she took healing like a dear little obedient child and fell into a sweet healing sleep. The apostle Paul says that he could hardly know what to choose, to depart and be with Christ, or stay in this sad world to help people here. But much as he longed to see Jesus, he chose to stay and do all he could to save and help (Philippians 1:21-25).

In the last chapter I told you how blessed it is to learn by heart Scripture verses on healing so that when we are tempted we can use them to inspire our faith. You know the Bible says that "above all" we must take "the shield of faith, wherewith ye shall be able to quench all the fiery darts of the wicked" (Ephesians 6:16). (It is "wicked one" in the Greek and means Satan.) And "faith cometh by hearing, and hearing by the word of God" (Romans 10:17).

I have asked a great many people to commit to memory the first seventeen verses of the eighth chapter of Matthew, for I have found that almost every question about healing is answered there. Also I have seen such wonderful healings where this Word is studied. In the Old Testament the animals that God called "clean" chewed the cud, as well as having divided hoofs. Doesn't that mean that we are to "chew" the Word of God? The first Psalm says that the "blessed" man "meditates" in God's Word day and night.

It is not hard to do that when you know it by heart. When you waken in the small hours of the morning and thoughts of difficult things in your life trouble you, just open your heart to the Holy Spirit by praises to God; and He will faithfully bring the Word you have learned to your remembrance. It will flow like a river of living water through your thoughts, driving doubt and fear away. Many of God's people have learned that sweet secret, and I want to teach it to you if you do not know it.

I am supposing that you have learned these verses, Matthew 8:1-17, and I am giving you some of the light and comfort people have found in them.

Verses 1-3. A poor leper came and worshiped Him. He would have been afraid to come near anyone else because his place was among the tombs. But he could not fear the Lord Jesus Christ. He is the Lamb of God. No one is afraid of a lamb. Even a child will hug a snowy lamb. Come to Jesus no matter how unworthy you feel. But the leper has a doubt: he knows that the Lord Jesus can heal him; somehow he cannot look into His eyes and doubt it. But *will* He? Tremblingly he says, "Lord, if thou wilt thou canst make me clean." Jesus snatches the "if" out of his mouth with His glad, "I will; be thou clean." And immediately his leprosy was cleansed, and it was a joyful man who went to the priest to receive his bill of health.

Do you ask, "Will He heal me?" You have His

answer, "I will." He tasted death for you as well as for the leper. He cannot say "Yes" to him, and "No" to you.

Then in verses 5 to 13, we have a very different case. The leper had "incomplete faith," which the Lord Jesus finished for He is the author and finisher of our faith (Hebrews 12:2), but the Roman centurion had "great faith." Jesus said so. Why was it so great? Because in spite of his unworthiness (he said, "I am not worthy"), he believed that Jesus would heal because He was Jesus. And he was sure that the word of Jesus had power to drive sickness away. Just as sure of that as he was that his servant would obey his orders. He knew everything had to obey the Lord Jesus.

Jesus said this Roman officer would sit down with Abraham, Isaac, and Jacob in the kingdom. Why? Because we sit down with our equals and all Abraham, Isaac, and Jacob did was to believe God's word. It is so easy to please God; only believe Him and He will do the rest. But without faith it is impossible to please Him (Hebrews 11:6). You can please Him if you will. Put away anything you know to be wrong ("They repented not that they might believe") and rest your heart on His promises. They cover your every need (Matthew 21:32).

In verses 14 and 15 the Lord enters Peter's humble home and finds the dear old grandmother very sick. Dr. Luke says she had a "high or great" fever (Luke 4:38). Peter's little house belongs to Jesus. Peter says he forsook all to follow the Lord. Everybody in the house is under the Master's special care. So Jesus touched the hand, hardened by much toil, and the fever left her and she rose to minister to Him and those with Him. Have you given your home and all your loved ones to Jesus? As the old hymn asks . . .

> Is your all on the altar of sacrifice laid,
>   Your heart does the Spirit control?
> You can only be blest
>   And have peace and sweet rest,
> As you yield Him your body and soul.

I once lived with some saints who had given their house and all who lived in it to the Lord. When three of their little children were very sick and it seemed sure that there would be death in the home, we prayed together. After we had done this I went to my room and there the Lord told me to give them the words, "I exhort you to be of good cheer for there shall be no loss of any man's life among you, but of the ship" (Acts 27:22). I had a fierce fight of faith before I was ready to give the message. From a medical viewpoint, death seemed certain for at least one of the little ones. The devil told me I would raise false hopes in their hearts and get into awful trouble myself. When I was ready to trust God, I said, "But Lord why should I say the words 'But of the ship'?" He said, "Give My message as I give it to you." I called them and solemnly told them what the Lord said. They received it as from God, and never had a shadow of a doubt. They did not seem to notice about the ship so I felt I must say, "But God told me I must say 'but of the Ship.'"

They were so happy about the children that they didn't seem to mind about the ship. Soon after they lost their house, but of course all the children got well and are living yet.

Now perhaps you will say, "I have not found a case like mine, yet, in this Scripture passage." Well, wait a moment and read verses 16 and 17: "When the even was come, they brought in to him many that were possessed with devils: and he cast out the spirits with his word and healed *all* that were sick: that it might be fulfilled which was spoken by Esaias the prophet, saying, Himself took our infirmities, and bare our sicknesses." (A quote from Isaiah 53:4.)

Here we see that He healed *all* that were sick, and you can't get outside of all; can you? And He did it because the Scripture cannot be broken, and it had been prophesied by Isaiah, seven hundred years before Christ came, that He would do just this. That Word still stands today.

6

Healing for Children

I know what mothers want to hear, and that is how to trust the Lord to keep the little ones well and strong. Also any who may have children who are not as sturdy as they should be want to know how to bring the little ones to the Great Physician and get them healed. There are no stories in the Bible, our book of instructions, sweeter than those that tell of the Lord Jesus' taking the little ones into His arms, laying His hands on them and blessing them. When I was working in a hospital in New York many years ago, I saw a beautiful oil painting — I think it was life size — which a very rich man gave. It almost filled the wall at one end of the ward. How the sick people loved to look at it, for it showed the Lord Jesus Christ bringing life and healing the little daughter of Jairus, a ruler of the synagogue.

The story is told three times in the New Testament: Matthew 9:18-26, Mark 5:22-46, and Luke 8: 40-56. I like to read about healings in Luke's Gospel, for he was himself a doctor and sometimes tells us things the others leave out.

In verse 41 we read that Jairus — who was a great man among the Jews, "a ruler of the synagogue" — came and fell down at the feet of Jesus and besought Him to come to his house. How simple his faith! How humble he was! While others were denying that Jesus was the Christ, this spiritual leader fell at His feet in public. It might cost him his job. Perhaps he would be put out of the synagogue of which he was a ruler. But he did not mind that. His only child, his darling daughter, a sweet damsel of twelve years lay dying. He knew in his soul that Jesus of Nazareth could save her life.

Perhaps it took that awful trial to bring the proud ruler to Jesus. I know a lovely young couple — educated, rich, but alas, without God — whose only child, a beautiful boy, lay dying. The family doctor held out no hope, but the baby's grandmother knew that Jesus is the same today; for she had been healed herself. And God gave her faith to go to her son and daughter and tell them that if they would fall at Jesus' feet and receive Him as their Saviour and Lord, the child would get well. She said, "The Lord told me to tell you this. If you do not surrender, the baby will die." They believed the Word and did just what Jairus did. And the child is a big boy now.

Jesus set out for Jairus' house, but a poor woman who had been sick many years and spent every cent on doctors, touched the hem of His garment and was made whole immediately. Then the Lord stopped the whole procession — there was a great crowd following Him — so that this woman could tell what had happened to her. How hard that was for the poor father!

Why was Jesus so anxious to let the woman speak? Perhaps so that her faith might be made strong and steadfast. Nothing helps you more than telling of His goodness and praising Him for His mercies. Then this wonderful healing of a hopeless case of twelve years' standing would help Jairus to believe that his daughter too would be healed. But some one came and said the little maid was dead. Even then the Lord Jesus told the father not to fear but believe. And when Jesus got to the beautiful home of Jairus — I am thinking of the picture I saw in the hospital — some people there wept and mourned, and others laughed Him to scorn. Jesus put them all out.

When I hear a person say, "Well they talk of healing by faith in the Lord Jesus Christ, but I never saw one," I cannot help thinking of the people who were put out. The Word of God does not promise that you will see if you are weeping and mourning, for *that* is unbelief. Do you dare to scorn the truth that Jesus Christ is the same today? He tells us the ones who will see His wonderful works, and they are those who believe. "Said I not unto thee that if thou wouldest believe thou shouldest see the glory of God?" Peter, James and John didn't weep and mourn. They knew too well the power of the Lord Jesus. The parents did not laugh Jesus to scorn. The father bowed himself at His feet. If you want to *see,* cease your mourning and fall at His feet in adoration. Oh, how sacred the hush that fell as the Lord stood beside the deathbed of the little maid and taking the cold limp hand in His (which had all power in heaven and earth) said tenderly, "Maid, arise." And she arose with shining face. Jesus, ever thoughtful, said to them, "Give her meat." Do you think that was strange? Not at all; I have seen people healed of sore sickness when their friends would ask half afraid, "Would it be right to give them something to eat?" It seemed too good to be true that they were really well and able to eat like other folks.

In the Gospel of John we have the story of the healing of the son of a nobleman who lived in the city of Capernaum, where a great many rich Romans had fine homes (John 4:46-54).

This case is very helpful to us for Jesus did not go to the child as He did to Jairus' daughter! He just spoke a word and the work was done because the child's father believed the word. We do not see the Lord Jesus walk in at the door when we pray to Him for our loved ones. But He is with us. He says, "I will never leave you nor forsake you" (Hebrews 13:5). We don't have to *send* for our Doctor. He says, "If a man love me, he will keep my words; and my Father will love him, and we will come unto him, and make our abode with him" (John 14:23).

The nobleman wanted Jesus to go to his house with all speed to heal his son who was at the point of death. But Jesus read his heart, and saw that he wanted to see something before he would believe. He had things turned the wrong way. We must believe that we may see. David says, "I had fainted, unless I had believed to see" (Psalm 27:13). "Faith is the evidence of things not seen" (Hebrews 11:1). The nobleman still pleaded for a visit from the Lord. He said, "Sir, come down ere my child die."

Then Jesus gave him a word, "Go thy way; thy son liveth." And the man believed the word that Jesus had spoken." And because believing the word of God is seeing, his son was healed.

When the children for whose healing we are praying are too young to take hold of the promise for themselves, we must get the parents to unite in faith for them. I have a big feather pillow made out of carefully selected feathers, which always reminds me of a tiny child I prayed for years ago at a camp meeting in Canada. She was terribly deaf as the result of scarlet fever. The mother, who was very anxious to have the Lord heal her little darling, brought her to the altar at a meeting and asked for prayer. I asked, "Is her father saved?" The mother, who was saved, seemed a little doubtful about it. "Well, go and tell him that I would like to see him. You must bring the child between you to the feet of Jesus." When they came with the little thing toddling between them, and together we bowed at the altar in simple faith in the Blood as our only plea, the child was instantly healed. I received the beautiful pillow and a homemade blanket as a thank offering. There was a note pinned to the pillow on which the child's name was written and a statement that she could hear a pin drop. I have always valued the pillow almost beyond anything I possess.

When children are old enough to believe for themselves, we must read the Word of God to them, especially stories about the healing Christ. "Faith cometh by hearing, and hearing by the word of God" (Romans 10:17). They are often more ready to believe than adults. Sometimes their faith helps older people to get well.

There is a hymn that we all love called, "God Will Take Care of You." I happened to hear from someone who knew all about how it came to be written and composed. A minister had been called to preach one Sunday in a large city and had brought his wife and little boy with him for the trip. They were at a hotel. Sunday morning, near church time, the minister's wife was taken very sick. She was so sick that the minister made up his mind to break his promise to preach, a thing he had never done in all his life. As he was going out of the door to take a message to the office, the tiny child ran over to his mother's bed and whispered in her ear, "Mother, God will take care of you." The childish faith stirred the mother to believe God, and she called her husband back. "Don't break your promise, dear," she said. "I would not have you do it for all the world. God will take care of me."

The minister's faith rose to meet the test and he went and did God's work. When he came back his wife met him with a smiling face and said, "God gave me a little hymn," and she read him the beautiful words:

> No matter what may be the test,
>   God will take care of you.
> Lean weary one, upon His breast,
>   God will take care of you.

The husband, who was a musician, sat down and played the sweet melody to which we sing it.

Children can often lead people to Christ for salvation and healing when older persons fail.

We have a wonderful story in the Old Testament (2 Kings 5:1-27), which tells how a little maid, who had been taken captive by the Syrians, was the means of healing the great Naaman, commander in chief of the army of the king of Syria. She was a servant to Naaman's wife; and when she saw that the commander was a leper, she said to her mistress in simple

faith in God, "Would God my lord were with the
prophet that is in Samaria! For he would recover him
of his leprosy." She was so sure that her faith moved
the great General Naaman, and even the king of Syria
who no doubt greatly longed to have his faithful general's life spared. If you read the story you will see
that the king of Syria wrote a letter to the king of Israel asking *him* to make Naaman well. That was not
what the little maid told them to do. She had said
that the prophet who was in Israel, Elisha, would
make Naaman well. Not because he had the power
himself but because God worked through him. Naaman took a great fortune with him, and costly rai-
ment, to buy his healing. That was not the little
maid's fault. She had said nothing about taking anything but himself, dying of a fatal disease for which
there was no human cure. When we come to Jesus
for healing we have to sing in our hearts:

> Just as I am without one plea,
>   But that Thy Blood was shed for me,
> And that Thou bidd'st me come to Thee
>   O Lamb of God I come.

Never forget that, "Jesus paid it all."

Naaman had to learn that the king of Israel could
not make him well; that all his money and rich gifts
could not help him at all. But one thing would heal
him, and that was the Word of God. That word was
spoken by Elisha, for he was God's mouthpiece. Naaman had to believe it. That was all. What did Elisha
say?

"Go and wash in Jordan seven times, and thy
flesh shall come again to thee, and thou shalt be
clean." He sent this word by a messenger. Naaman

didn't have any chance to show what a great officer he was, how many servants he had, or to present his costly gifts.

He was angry. No doubt he said to himself, "The prophet turns me away like a beggar." That was all he was. Just a poor beggar, with his flesh falling off his bones from leprosy. Sometimes God has to bring us down very low before He can heal us. But thank God, Naaman believed the word enough to obey it to the letter. Down he went seven times and received such a wonderful healing! His flesh that had sloughed off came again as fresh as a little child's.

The Lord Jesus Christ used Naaman's case to teach the people in His home town, Nazareth, what real faith meant (Luke 4:27). And it all came about through the faith of a little captive girl. How happy she must have been when her master, the splendid Generalissimo Naaman, came marching home to his wife and children, as well as to his king and country.

I could tell you many stories out of my own life where children, even tiny ones have been used in the Lord's healing. I think I shall tell you a funny one here and hope you will read it to your little ones if you are so happy as to have some.

We had a beautiful fox terrier puppy given to us, a fine dog and very bright — almost too bright for us. So we decided to give him to a sister who had a number of children who loved to play with him. She was glad to have him. One day she noticed that the puppy was sick. She told the children that they were not to play with him or even touch him. He had run under the big kitchen range after refusing to eat.

She noticed that the children — she had them of all ages down to three — went into a huddle and talked very earnestly. The one who was only three years old took a very active part in the discussion. Then she saw them all go to a corner and kneel down. They stayed there some time.

Then they came out in a solemn little procession and said, "Mother, we have prayed for Puppy and we are sure he is well. You said that when he was well he would come running when we called him, wagging his tail, and would eat his breakfast. And you said too that his nose would be cold. May we call him to his breakfast? We know he will come running and wagging his tail. And, Mother, may we just touch the tip of his nose, just barely touch it. We are sure it is cold as ice." As she hesitated one of them offered the crowning argument by saying, "Mother, you said that God blessed His people's cattle and kept them well. He is our cattle, isn't he?"

Rather weakly she said, "Well, you may call him." This was done in a chorus and the dog ran out wagging his tail and rushed to his breakfast plate. Then one of the children cried, "O Mother I just touched his nose the least teeny-weeny bit and it is cold as an icicle."

I think this story shows that we are not to despise the faith of children, even tiny ones, but try to encourage it all we can.

Perhaps I might tell one more case of victory through the faith of a little child. The father of the child, who is a man of God, is my authority. The child's mother suffered for years from neuralgia in her face. The child, a little girl, loved her mother dearly, and when she had these awful attacks she suffered with her. She was taught and believed that the Lord Jesus bore our pains on the Cross. One day — I think she was five years old at the time — while her mother was in awful agony she jumped up and ran to her and laid her hands on her *in faith*. That was the last attack.

Faith is faith, whether in children or adults, and faith is the victory that overcomes.

7

You Have Authority

Supposing we consider healings that happened after the Lord Jesus Christ led His apostles out to Mount Olivet, a short distance from Jerusalem, and was caught up to heaven, a cloud receiving Him out of their sight.

How hard it was for them to see Him vanish from their eyes! But God gave them one great comfort. What was it? He sent two messengers to say, "This same Jesus, which is taken up from you into heaven, shall so come in like manner as ye have seen him go into heaven" (Acts 1:11).

This is the blessed hope of all God's dear children. I am sure that it reminded the disciples that their Master, who was coming again, had left them some work to do for Him. Don't you think it ought to make us all pray, "Lord, what wilt thou have me to do?" (Acts 9:6).

What had the Lord told them to do? You will find it in Luke 24:49: "Behold I send the promise of mv

Father upon you; but tarry ye in the city of Jerusalem, until ye be endured with power from on high."

They remembered His words (Acts 1:12), and we find them returning to Jerusalem to an upper room, where with other disciples — 120 in all — they continued in prayer until the Promise of the Father, the gift of the Holy Spirit, came upon them all and they began to speak in other tongues as the Spirit gave them utterance (Acts 2:4).

Have you obeyed that command of the Lord Jesus Christ yet? If not, lose no time about it for His coming draweth nigh! "The promise is unto you, and to your children . . . even as many as the Lord our God shall call" (Acts 2:39).

They needed the Holy Spirit in those days but not any more than we need Him in these days. They were His witnesses for that time, and we are His witnesses for this time.

Very soon after this we find the mighty power of the Holy Spirit shown in the healing of a most desperate case (Acts 3:1-16). For years and years a poor man had been laid each day at the Beautiful Gate of the temple in Jerusalem. There good people, who might give him alms as they entered that holy place to pray, would be sure to see him lying helpless, for he had never walked. He had been born a cripple. He was forty years old at the time of which we are talking.

It seems almost certain that the Lord Jesus Christ had seen him, for we know that Jesus loved to go to the temple because it was His Father's house. Why did not the Lord Jesus heal him? We do not know the answer to that question, for the Bible does not tell us. Perhaps the poor cripple had not yet come to the place of repentance and faith. It may be that the crucifixion of the Lord on Calvary and His Resurrection from the dead brought faith to the heart of the poor sufferer. He would be sure to hear of these things, for they were noised abroad all over the holy city.

The Lord Jesus had made the healing of the cripple possible before He left for His heavenly home, for He had told His disciples that they were to lay hands on sick people in His Name and that the sick people would get well (Mark 16:15-18).

And so that they would not be afraid to do this, He said to them, "Verily, verily, I say unto you, He that believeth on me, the works that I do shall he do also; and greater works than these shall he do; because I go unto my Father" (John 14:12).

Did the Lord Jesus ever heal a lame man? Yes, many of them. We are told that the lame came to Him in the temple, at the gate of which the cripple lay, and He healed them there. And in many other places besides, He made the lame to walk. One man who had lain for thirty-eight years, helpless to move himself, got up and took up his bed and walked at the Word of the Lord. That story is in John 5:1-9.

So when the apostles, Peter and John, saw this lame man reaching out his empty hand – all he could move – and asking for an alms, they remembered the words of the Lord. And Peter fastened his eyes on him with John. Oh, how we need to work *together* in healing! And he commanded, "Look on us." Whether you get healed or not depends *entirely* on where you look. If that man had fixed his gaze on his legs (mere bags of skin and bone, for they had never been used, and the muscles had not grown), he would not have been healed no matter how earnestly the apostles had prayed for him. Jesus Himself, "did not many mighty works" in His own home town. Why? Because of their unbelief. It is "according to your faith"; the Lord Himself said so. When the brazen serpent was lifted up on a pole in the wilderness by Moses at God's command to heal the stricken Israelites who were bitten by fiery serpents, we are told that if a serpent had bitten any man, when he beheld the serpent of brass, he lived. Not when he was looking at his sore wounds but when he fixed his eyes on God's cure for them — the brazen serpent (Numbers 21:8, 9).

The brazen serpent is a picture of the Lord Jesus made sin for us, that we might be made the righteousness (rightness) of God in Him. The Lord Himself says so in John 3:14, 15: "As Moses lifted up the serpent in the wilderness, even so must the Son of man be lifted up; that whosoever believeth in Him should not perish, but have eternal life."

Here we have the lame man looking at Peter and John, messengers of the Lord Jesus, and "expecting to receive something of them." I am sure he did not expect what he got. God is able to give us exceeding abundantly above all we can ask or expect and He loves to do it. Our part is to look away from everything else to Jesus, and if we do that we cannot expect too much.

Peter said, "Silver and gold have I none; but such as I have give I thee." He had no money; he said so. But he still had something to give. What was that something? Had he some magic power perhaps granted him because he had left all to follow Christ? In verse 12 he says he had no power of his own to cure the man. Yet he gave him something that made that cripple leap up, stand, and walk into the temple leaping and praising God.

What was that something? Three times over he tells us that it was the power of the Name of Jesus Christ of Nazareth. He explains exactly how it was done, "through *faith in His Name*" (Acts 3:6, 16; 4:10).

Once for some time I held a government position where I had the right to sign the name of a high officer which carried with it power to enforce obedience. Because of this, the orders I sent out had to be obeyed. I had no power of my own, and if I had used my own name no one would have moved an inch.

I did many things of great value to many people. But it was all through the power of the name I was told to use. If I had not had faith in that name I would not have been able to do these things, because I would not have used it. If I had not used it, I would have disobeyed.

What Peter had was power to use the Name that is above every name. The Name that has to be obeyed. He was not only allowed to use it, but it was his duty to do so. The Lord Jesus had said to Peter and the others, "In my name, shall they lay hands on the sick and they shall recover" (Mark 16:17, 18).

He was telling them and us to preach the gospel to every creature, so this Word is to us today. To whom? "Them that believe." If we do not use this Name, it is because we are not believing what Jesus said.

This wonderful healing of the lame man led to many, many healings and signs and wonders. They even brought the sick ones out into the streets and laid them on beds and couches so that Peter's shadow might fall on them. A great many people believed and were added to the church. Also awful persecution arose. Satan did not like these healings because he hates to see the glorious Name of the Lord Jesus Christ praised and worshipped. He does not like divine healing any better today. But the apostles and early Christians went right along doing what the Lord had told them to do, and the Lord went with them doing miracles. Shall we follow our Lord and Master as closely as they did? If we do we may count on His power.

Not long after this miracle of the lame man at the temple gate Peter went down to a place called Lydia. There he found a man called Aeneas, who was paralyzed and had been bedfast for eight long years. How he must have suffered! I have seen so many sad cases like his, and my heart went out to them; but there was nothing I could do for them though I was a doctor. Peter was no doctor; but, as we saw in the story of the lame man, he had something to give — if they would take it — that made sick people perfectly sound.

Knowing that the medicine never failed, he said "Aeneas, Jesus Christ maketh thee whole! Arise! And make thy bed." And he arose immediately. What was the use of lying round another moment? He had had enough of that to last him a lifetime.

Has that medicine lost its power? No; and it will never fail, for it is the power of the Name of the Lord Jesus Christ. And we read in Psalm 72:17: "His name shall endure for ever: . . . and men shall be blessed in him; all nations shall call him blessed."

Let us use that Name in faith.

8

The Joy of the Lord

When you have a sure cure for all disease, you only need one remedy. "Who forgiveth all thine iniquities; who healeth all thy diseases" (Psalm 103:3). It is because doctors have no medicine that will cure every disease that they are always working so hard trying to find new remedies. Then the medicines they have are more or less uncertain in their action. They do not always do what the doctors expect.

But when the medicine is God's Word, it cannot fail. He says about it: "So shall my word be that goeth forth out of my mouth: it shall not return unto me void, but it shall accomplish that which I please, and it shall prosper in the thing whereto I sent it" (Isaiah 55:11). So when God sends His Word to heal you, it always does its work if you will let it.

"Can I prevent it from healing me?" Certainly you can. God does not force salvation for soul or body upon us. It is written, "whosoever will, let him take of the water of life freely" (Revelation 22:17).

To get the action of any remedy you have to take that remedy according to directions. Sometimes when I was practicing medicine, I would go to see a sick person and leave them a prescription to be taken according to instructions. When I returned I would see at a glance — for I knew what the medicine would do if they took it — that they had not taken it according to directions. When they saw that I was angry with them, they would sometimes say they had taken it. Then I was angry for sure!

God says that He sends His Word and heals. His Word cannot fail, so if we are not healed we must look for the cause of it in ourselves. It must be that we have not taken it according to instructions. What is lacking? Turn to the Bible and you will find out. In Hebrews 4:2 it says, "The word preached did not profit them, not being mixed with faith in them that heard it." To take the Word, you must mix it with faith. The Lord Jesus Himself said when healing two blind men, "According to your faith be it unto you" (Matthew 9:29).

One thing the Bible tells us about our wonderful bodies is that to keep them healthy, well oiled, running smoothly, we have to be happy. It is our duty to be happy. God commands it. You will find this in many places in the Bible, our book of instructions. In the prophecy of Joel, 2:21, we read, "Be glad and rejoice." That is a command of God. Then in Nehemiah 8:10, we find it given again in the negative form. Joel tells us what we must do, and Nehemiah tells us what we must not do. "Neither be ye sorry; for the joy of the Lord is your strength."

Oh, what a difference it would make if all God's people would obey these commands!

There is a great power in happiness. When I practiced medicine I had a great many baby cases. That means I was often with mothers to welcome the precious little ones God gave them. I always wanted my mothers and babies to be well and strong, and I found that the best tonic I could give the mothers was their babies. Some doctors had them taken away to a nursery in the hospital to be cared for by nurses, but I was not so fond of that. Looking at their babies and listening to their voices made my little mothers very happy, and happiness is the best tonic I know. If human happiness makes us strong, what will the joy the Bible speaks of do? This joy is as far above earthly joys and pleasures as the heavens are high above the earth. God wants us to have it constantly. He even tells us that we shall be punished if we are not happy. And one of the punishments He speaks of is sickness.

"Because thou servedst not the Lord thy God with joyfulness, and with gladness of heart, for the abundance of all things; therefore shalt thou serve thine enemies which the Lord shall send against thee. . . . Moreover He will bring upon thee all the diseases of Egypt, which thou wast afraid of; and they shall cleave unto thee. Also every sickness, and every plague, which is not written in . . . this law, them will the Lord bring upon thee" (Deuteronomy 28:47, 48, 60, 61).

How are we to get this joy that makes our hearts rejoice and our bodies strong? God has provided it for us and tells us how to get it in the book of instructions — the Bible.

David says, "I will go unto the altar of God, unto God my exceeding joy" (Psalm 43:4).

Peter tells us about it: "Whom having not seen, ye

love; in whom, though now ye see him not, yet believing, ye rejoice with joy unspeakable and full of glory" (1 Peter 1:8).

Believing what the Bible says about the Lord Jesus and what He has done for you and yours, you *rejoice, you just can't help it*. And you are strong, for the "joy of the Lord is your strength." Believing you rejoice, but doubting you despair and become weak and ready to fall a victim to sickness.

There is only one thing that will give you this wonderful joy that fills your soul and spirit with glory and makes your very "bones rejoice," and that is faith in the Lord Jesus Christ and what He did for you when He died on the Cross *for you*, and rose again, showing that *your* "old account" was settled.

Money cannot give you this joy. It is not to be bought for gold. You may have kind friends who would be glad to help you in every way possible, but they cannot bestow this gladness upon you. It has to come down from heaven, for "Every perfect gift is from above, and cometh down from the Father of lights" (James 1:17). On the other hand, nothing can take this joy from you, for He says of the joy He gives us, "Your joy no man taketh from you" (John 16:22).

We are living in awful days, and we need the joy of the Lord as much, or more, than any of His children ever needed it. For a great many years I have received letters from people asking for prayer and counsel. But the letters that have come to me of late have been the saddest I have ever received. Some of them are so sad that I hasten to destroy them when I have prayed over them for fear anyone might happen to see them and be saddened by them. When I get these letters, I am so glad that I have the "gladdest letter" that ever was written. It is in my Bible. I hasten to drink of its sweetness and to pass the sparkling cup to the poor sufferers to whom I am writing. I know you are asking, "Where is that gladdest of all letters?" Was it written by someone who had everything heart could wish and was surrounded by loved ones and shielded from every danger?"

It was written by a man nearing seventy, in a dark, damp, slimy cellar under the city of Rome, Italy. A man who had "suffered the loss of all things." He was the prisoner of the Emperor Nero, the most awful monster that ever lived, and was chained to a Roman soldier. He was so filled with joy that his praises have rung down all the years and changed wails of woe to songs of victory in countless hearts, since he went home to glory. That man is the apostle Paul, and the "gladdest letter" ever written, all "joy unspeakable and full of glory," is his Epistle to the "saints in Christ Jesus . . . at Philippi." Thank God, it is ours as well as theirs!

I do not believe we begin to know what a mighty thing the joy of the Lord is, to keep us well and heal us, if we are sick. I am going to relate a *joy* healing that comes to me at this time. It happened at least six years ago in Chicago, where I was holding a campaign for Brother S. A. Jamieson. As though to freshen my mind as to all the details, the minister who with me visited the sick man, happened to call upon me not long ago. I had not seen him for a long time until then. Of course we talked over this case. He was acting as pastor of a congregation in Chicago, and the sick man attended his church. When we reached

the home, which was in a humble little flat, we saw
one of the saddest scenes we had ever seen. The
young couple was only recently married. They were
sweet Christian people. Though the furniture was
not fine, everything was just as neat as it could be.
But the faces of those dear young people, I shall
never forget. He was very, very sick, with that pale,
drawn, anxious look that comes with awful suffering.
His case was stone in the kidney and he had the usual anguish, bleeding, etc., that goes with it. He was
booked for an operation in a day or so. The little wife
knelt at the foot of the bed. She had her face buried
in the coverlet, to hide her tears from her husband I
suppose. And I noticed that her hands clasped his
feet as though to prevent anyone from taking him
away. I knew what that meant: the ambulance. She
was thinking of the moment it would stop at their
door.

Nothing could be sadder than this case, yet the
Lord Jesus was so manifestly present that it seemed
the man's healing was inevitable. We read about the
Lord in the Word and He seemed to step out of it and
stand in our midst. Never shall I forget the joy of
that hour! We were in the heavenlies, anxiety was
impossible in that atmosphere. We just adored Him
to our heart's content. All the pale, drawn look of
anguish vanished from the young husband's face, and
he laughed and laughed and laughed and *laughed!*
The little wife joined in silvery notes, and it was a
laughing duet. We lost our sense of time and place.
Like Peter on the Mount of Transfiguration we were
only conscious that it was good for us to be there.

I know that the song in our hearts was

Oh, it is Jesus, Oh, it is Jesus, Oh, it is Jesus in my soul,
  For I have touched the hem of His garment,
And His power has made me whole.

The young husband was healed and went to
church and gave God the glory.

9

The Lord's Prayer

While writing these little chapters I have thought so much of you my readers that you have become very dear to me. I see mothers who feel too weak to bear the heavy burdens that life brings, seeking strength in these pages.

Tiny children, with eyes too large for their pale wasted little faces, seem to be looking to me for aid. Fathers of families too, crushed under sickness which makes it impossible for them to earn for their loved ones what they need, are asking, "Is there healing and health for me?" Yes. God, who changeth not, has promised to heal all who call upon Him in the *name of the Lord Jesus Christ.*

In closing I desire to point out to you that in the Lord's Prayer which our Lord Jesus Himself taught us to pray, there is a plea for healing and health in every clause. Let us read it from Matthew 6:9-13.

Our Father which art in Heaven. Who is our Father? If we have been born again, "The Lord that healeth thee" (Exodus 15:26).

Hallowed be Thy name. For what does His Name stand? "His name through faith in his name hath made this man strong, whom ye see and know; yea, the faith, which is by him hath given him . . . perfect soundness" (Acts 3:16).

Thy kingdom come. This is a prayer for health of body, as well as spirit. We are told that "Of the increase of his government and peace there shall be no end" (Isaiah 9:7). God has promised to keep us in perfect peace if we trust in Him (Isaiah 26:3). Perfect peace means perfect health of body as well as mind. The Lord Jesus is the Prince of Peace (Isaiah 9:6).

Thy will be done in earth, as it is in heaven. There is no sickness in heaven. In Revelation 21:4 we read, "And God shall wipe away all tears from their eyes; and there shall be no more death, neither sorrow, nor crying, neither shall there be any more pain."

Give us this day our daily bread. Here we are praying for physical as well as spiritual blessing. The Lord Jesus Christ Himself speaks of healing as the "children's bread" (Matthew 15:26). In praying for our daily bread we are asking for perfect health. It is only if we have this that we can be properly nourished by our food.

And forgive us our debts (or sins). In the 5th chapter of Luke's Gospel, the Lord Jesus Christ said that He healed the paralytic, who was borne of four men, "that ye may know that the Son of man hath power upon earth to forgive sins." Forgiveness and healing go together. When the sin is pardoned and put away, the mortgage on the house — our bodies — is lifted.

Lead us not into temptation. I do not know any temptations that are harder to fight than those of doubt, fear, unbelief, discouragement and despair, that come with Satan's attacks on our bodies.

Deliver us from evil. This covers all diseases, for they are mentioned as part of the curse of the broken Law.

We are sure of the answer to this prayer . . . "for thine is the kingdom, and the power, and the glory, for ever, amen."